Preschool | Kindergarten | 1st Grade   Beginning Writer Series

Writing Numbers 1-20

Macy McCullough

Trace the number 1.

1 1 1 1 1 1

one one one

1 1 1 1 1 1

one one one

1 1 1 1 1 1

one one one

Trace the number 1.

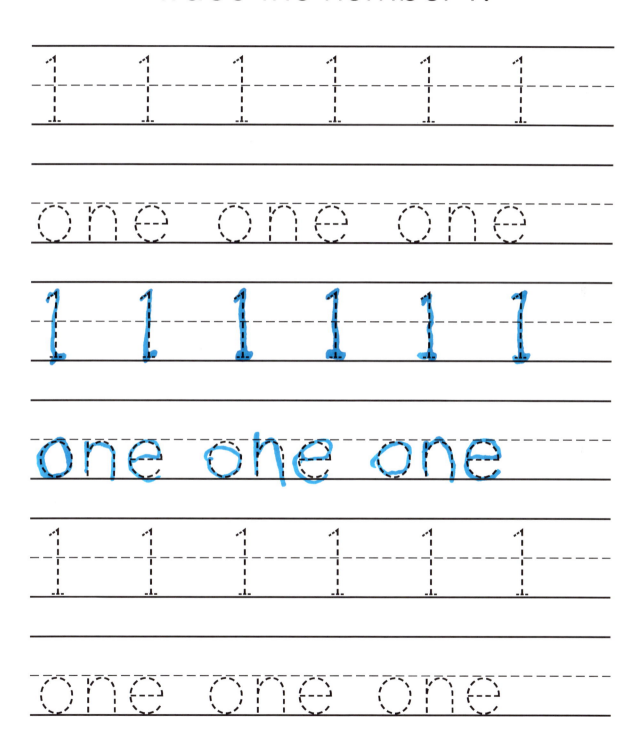

Practice writing the number 1.

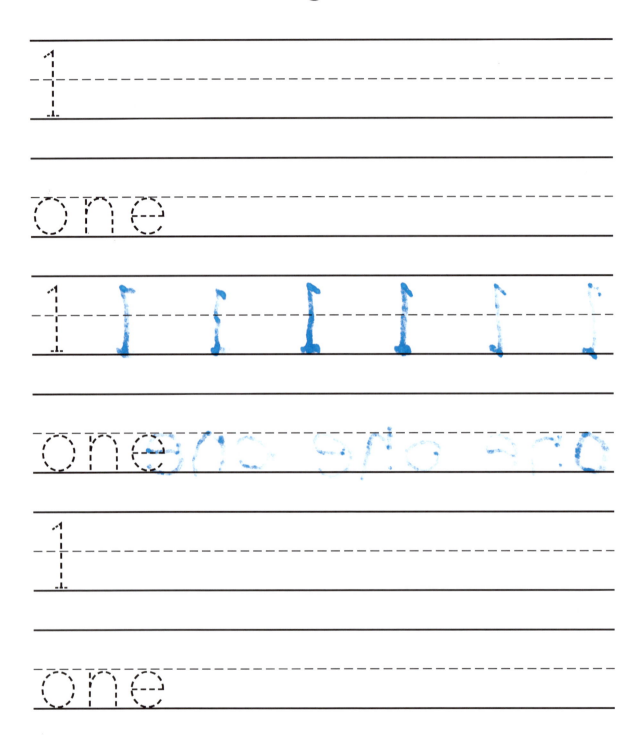

Practice writing the number 1.

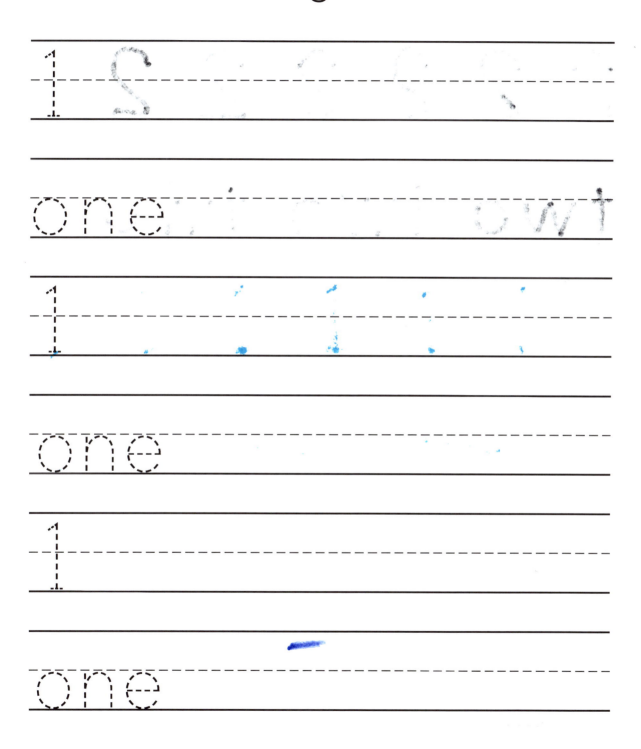

Trace the number 2.

2 2 2 2 2 2

two two two

2 2 2 2 2 2

two two two

2 2 2 2 2 2

two two two

Trace the number 2.

2 2 2 2 2

two two two

2 2 2 2 2 2

two two two

2 2 2 2 2 2

two two two

Practice writing the number 2.

2

two

2

two

2

two

Practice writing the number 2.

2

two

2

two

2

two

Trace the number 3.

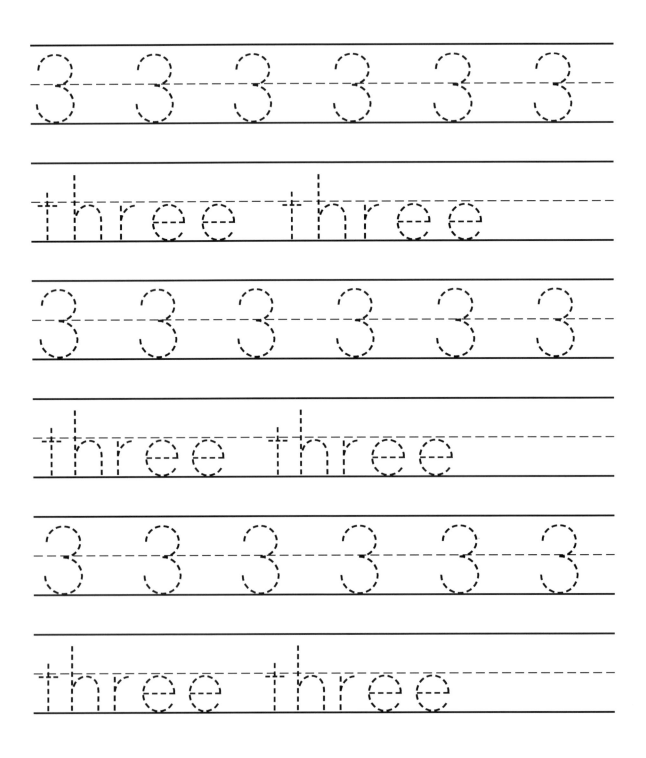

Trace the number 3.

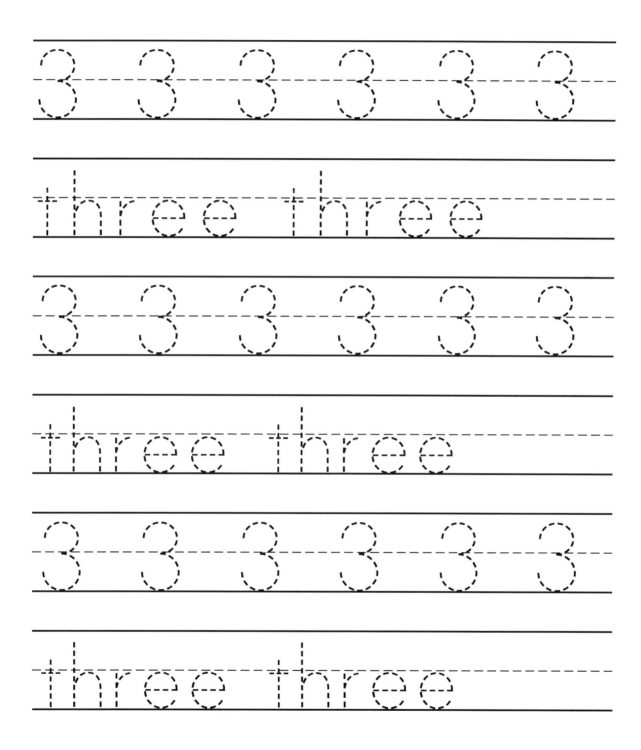

Practice writing the number 3.

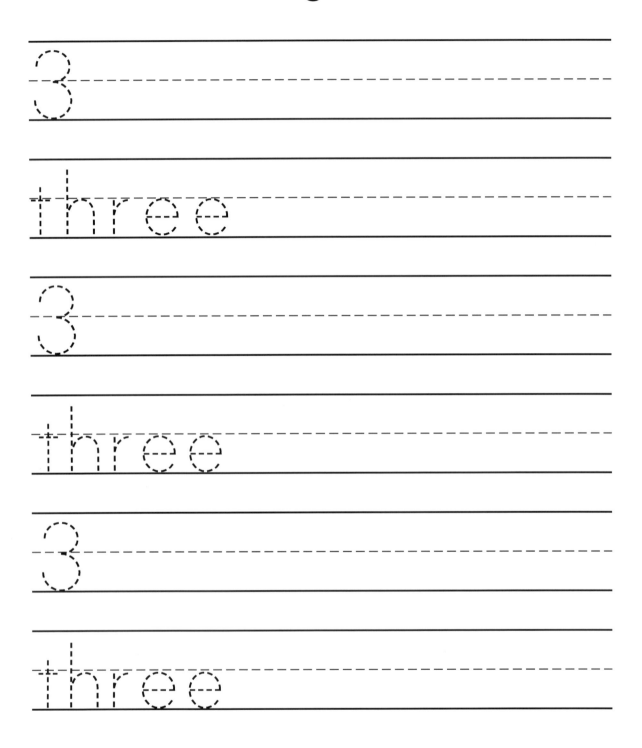

Practice writing the number 3.

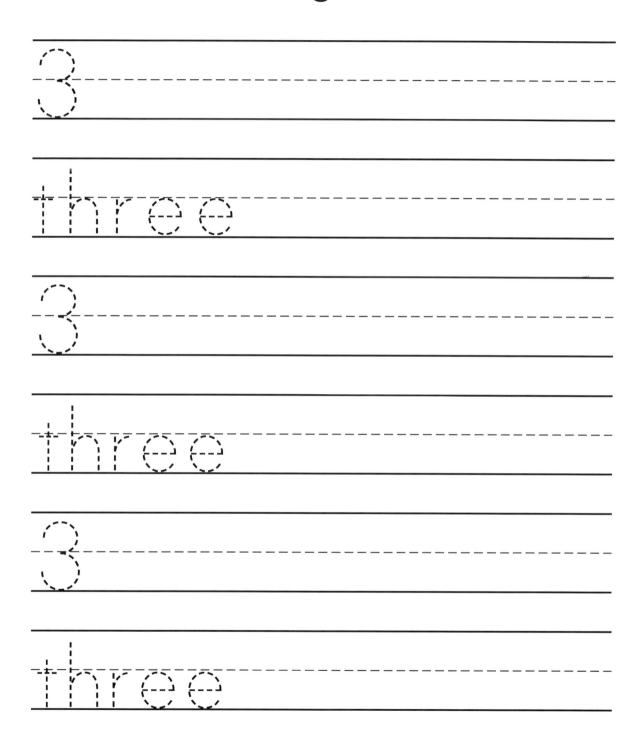

Trace the number 4.

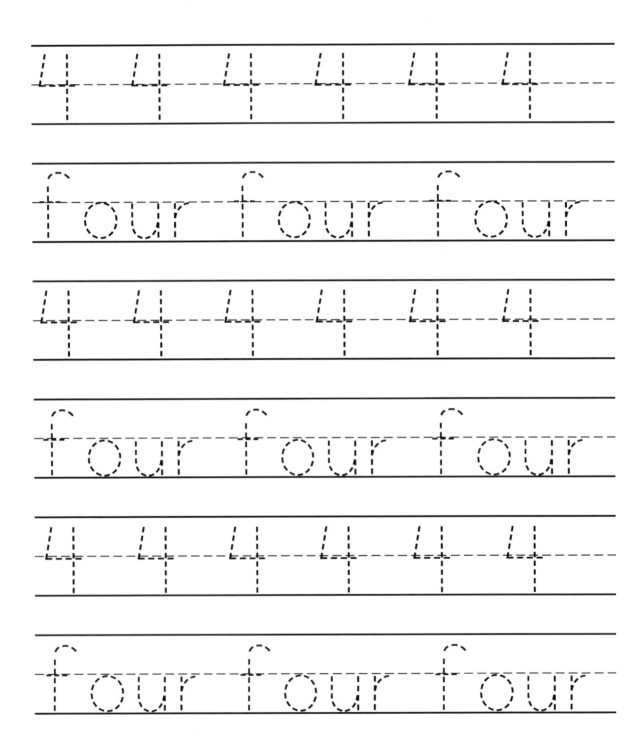

Trace the number 4.

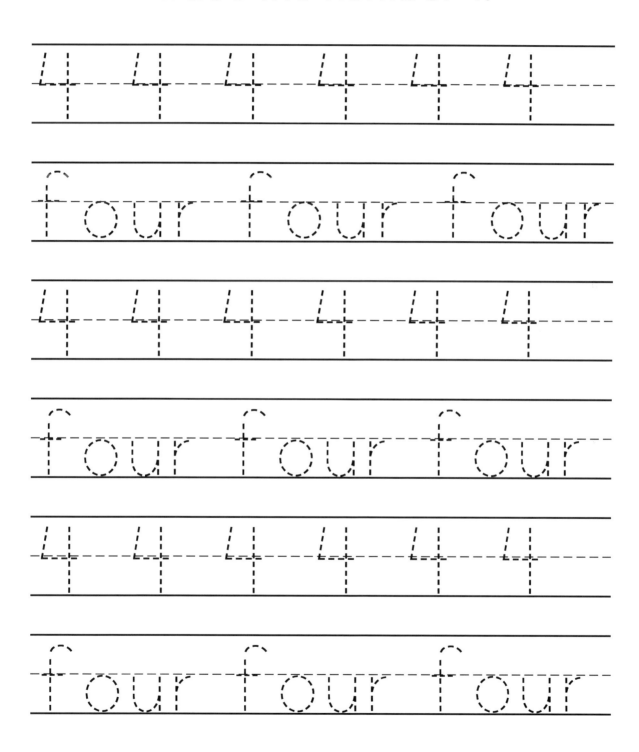

Practice writing the number 4.

4

four

4

four

4

four

Practice writing the number 4.

Trace the number 5.

Trace the number 5.

5 5 5 5 5 5

five five five

5 5 5 5 5 5

five five five

5 5 5 5 5 5

five five five

Practice writing the number 5.

5

five

5

five

5

five

Practice writing the number 5.

5

five

5

five

5

five

Trace the number 6.

Trace the number 6.

Practice writing the number 6.

6

six

6

six

6

six

Practice writing the number 6.

6

six

6

six

6

six

Trace the number 7.

7 7 7 7 7

seven   seven

7 7 7 7 7

seven   seven

7 7 7 7 7

seven   seven

Trace the number 7.

7 7 7 7 7

seven seven

7 7 7 7 7

seven seven

7 7 7 7 7

seven seven

Practice writing the number 7.

7

seven

7

seven

7

seven

Practice writing the number 7.

7

seven

7

seven

7

seven

Trace the number 8.

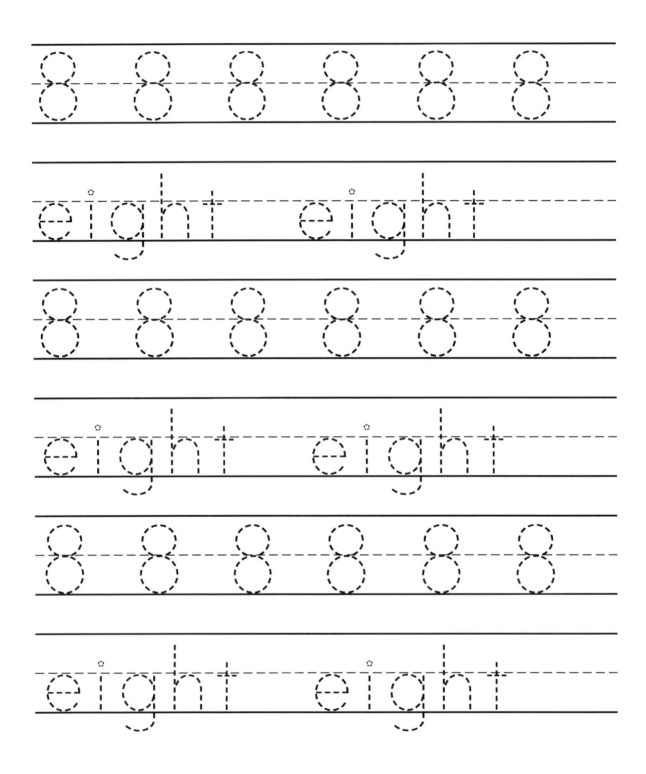

Trace the number 8.

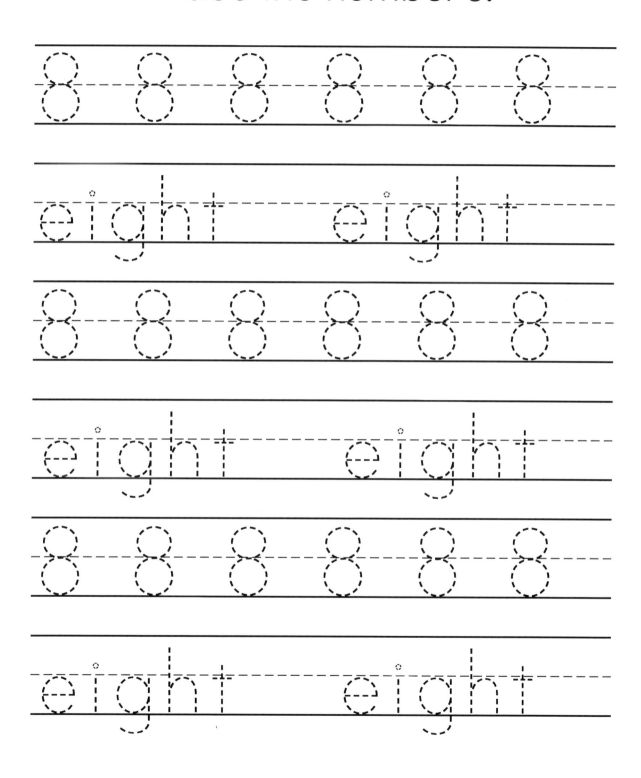

Practice writing the number 8.

Practice writing the number 8.

Trace the number 9.

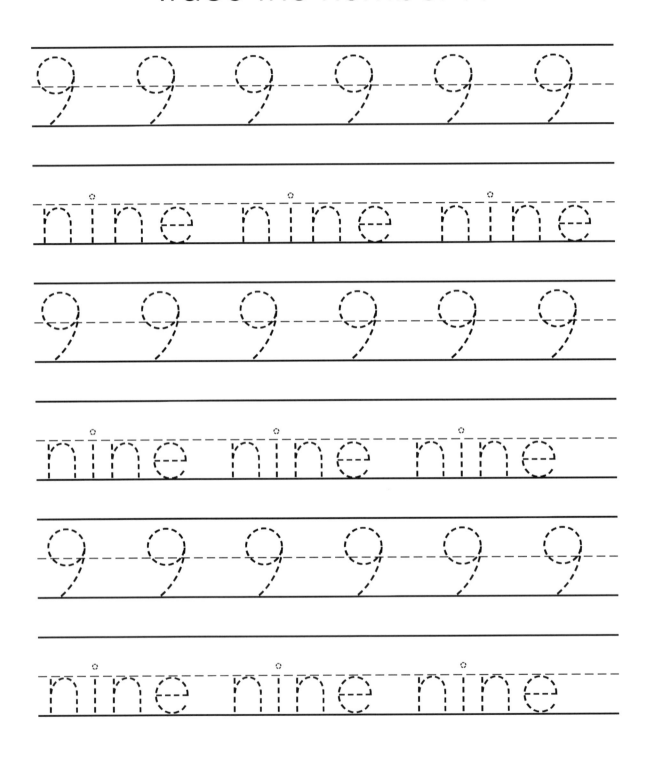

Trace the number 9.

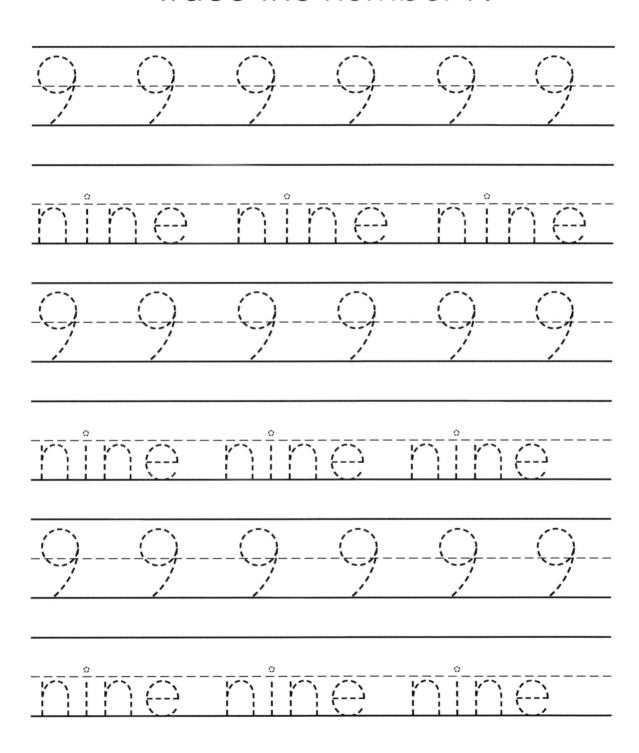

Practice writing the number 9.

9

nine

9

nine

9

nine

Practice writing the number 9.

9

nine

9

nine

9

nine

Trace the number 10.

10 10 10 10

ten ten ten ten

10 10 10 10

ten ten ten ten

10 10 10 10

ten ten ten ten

Trace the number 10.

10 10 10 10

ten ten ten ten

10 10 10 10

ten ten ten ten

10 10 10 10

ten ten ten ten

Practice writing the number 10.

10

ten

10

ten

10

ten

Practice writing the number 10.

10

ten

10

ten

10

ten

Trace the number 11.

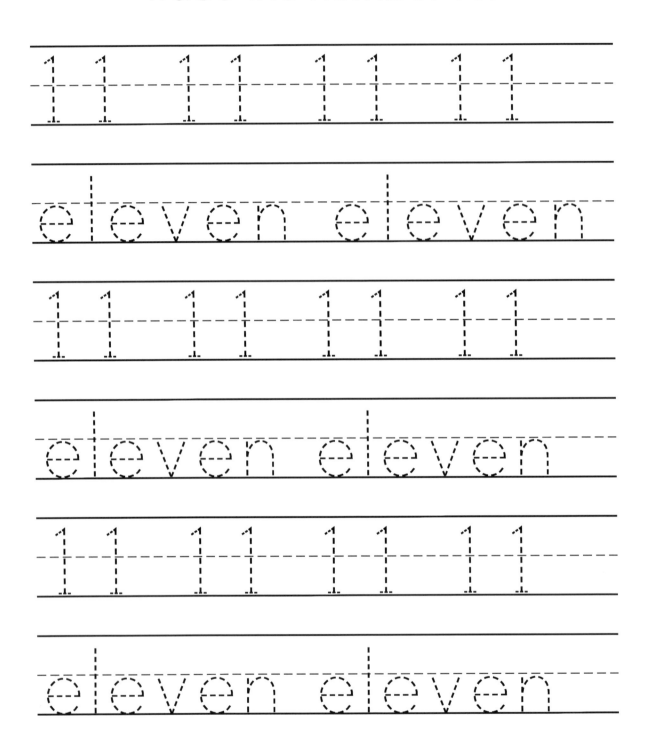

Trace the number 11.

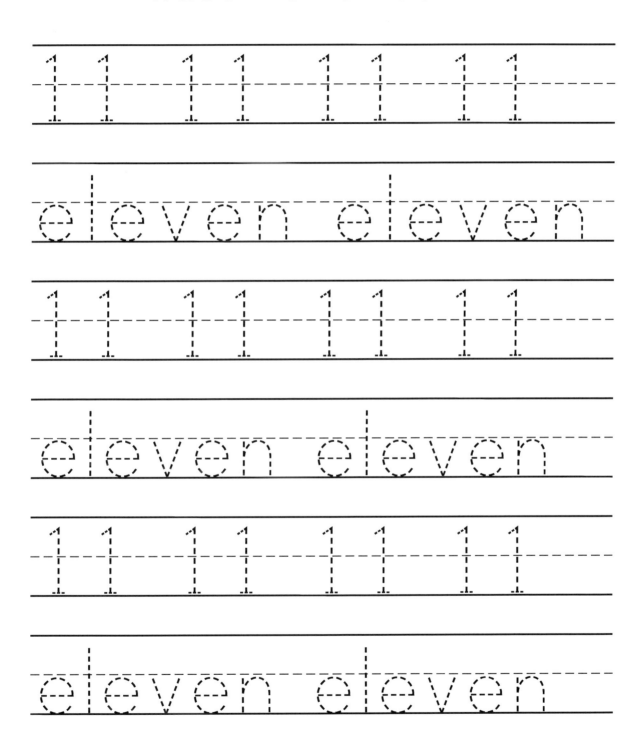

Practice writing the number 11.

Practice writing the number 11.

1 1

eleven

1 1

eleven

1 1

eleven

Trace the number 12.

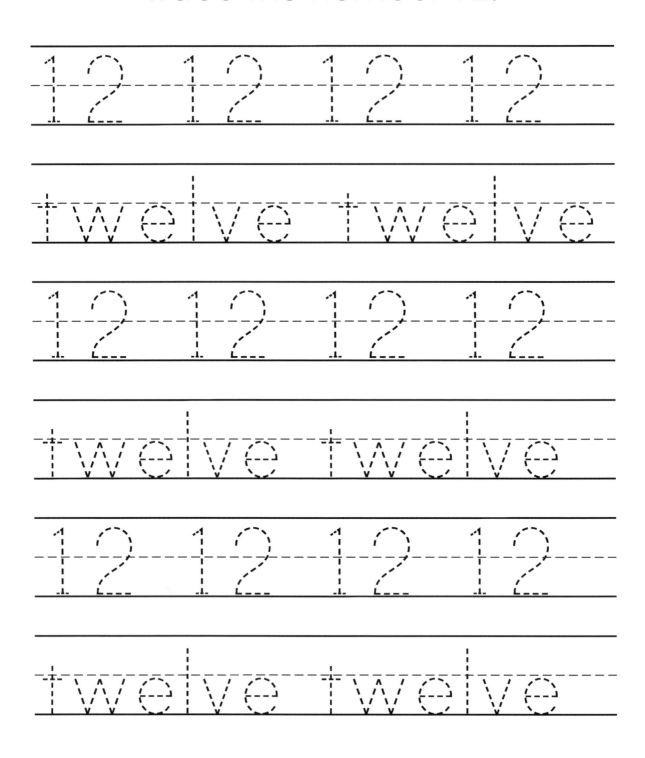

Trace the number 12.

12 12 12 12

twelve twelve

12 12 12 12

twelve twelve

12 12 12 12

twelve twelve

Practice writing the number 12.

Practice writing the number 12.

Trace the number 13.

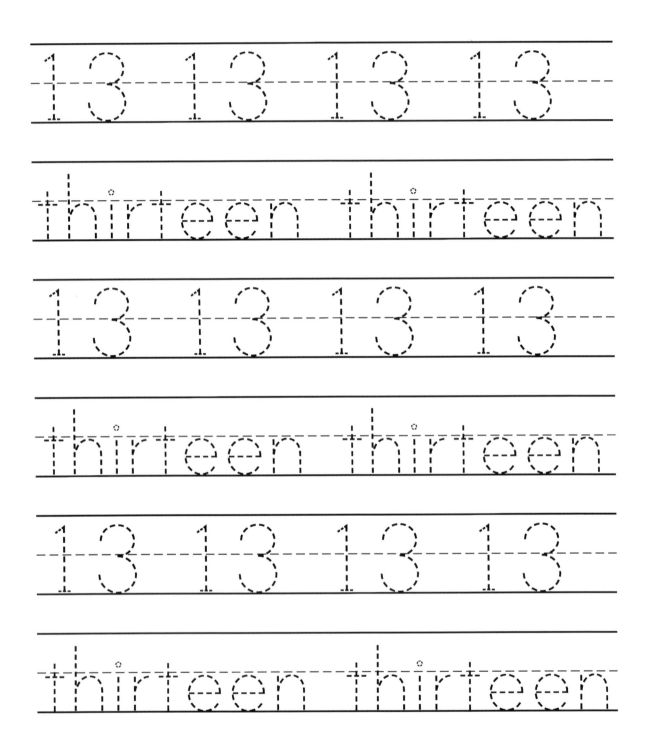

Trace the number 13.

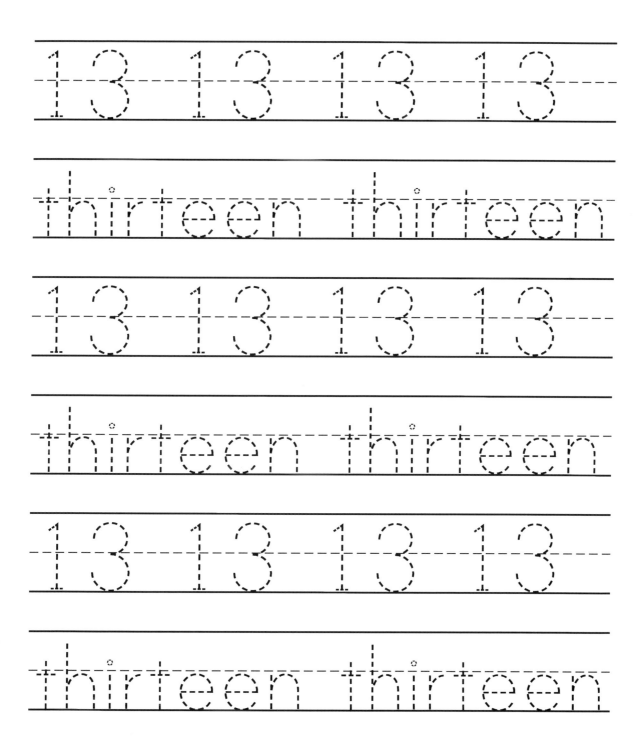

Practice writing the number 13.

Practice writing the number 13.

Trace the number 14.

14 14 14 14

fourteen fourteen

14 14 14 14

fourteen fourteen

14 14 14 14

fourteen fourteen

Trace the number 14.

14 14 14 14

fourteen fourteen

14 14 14 14

fourteen fourteen

14 14 14 14

fourteen fourteen

Practice writing the number 14.

14

fourteen

14

fourteen

14

fourteen

Practice writing the number 14.

14

fourteen

14

fourteen

14

fourteen

Trace the number 15.

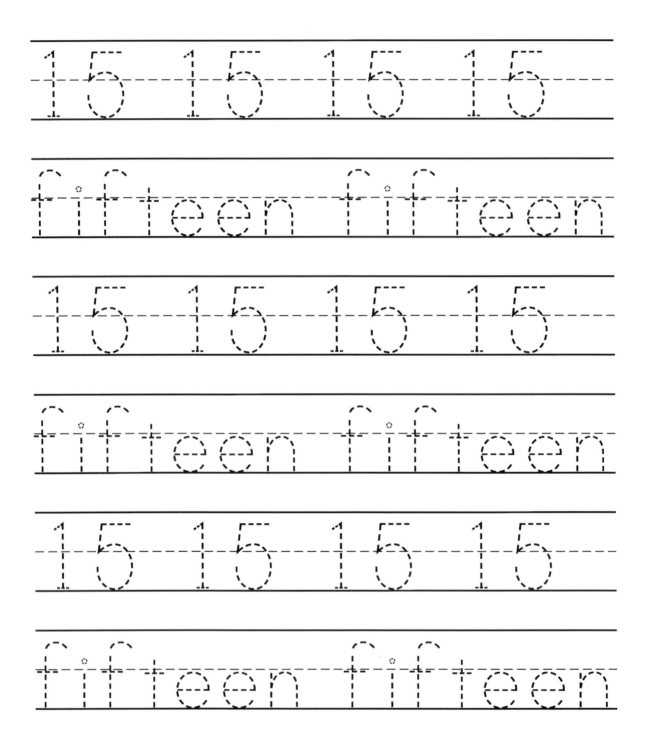

Trace the number 15.

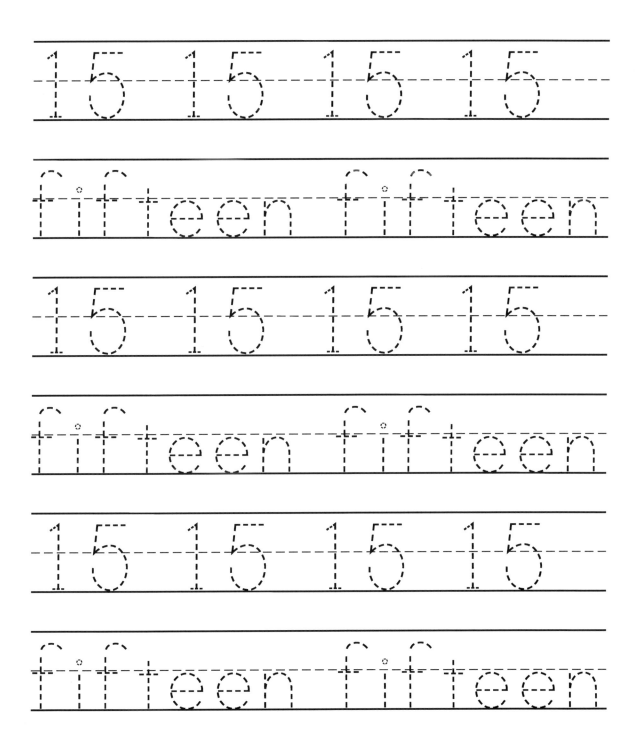

Practice writing the number 15.

Practice writing the number 15.

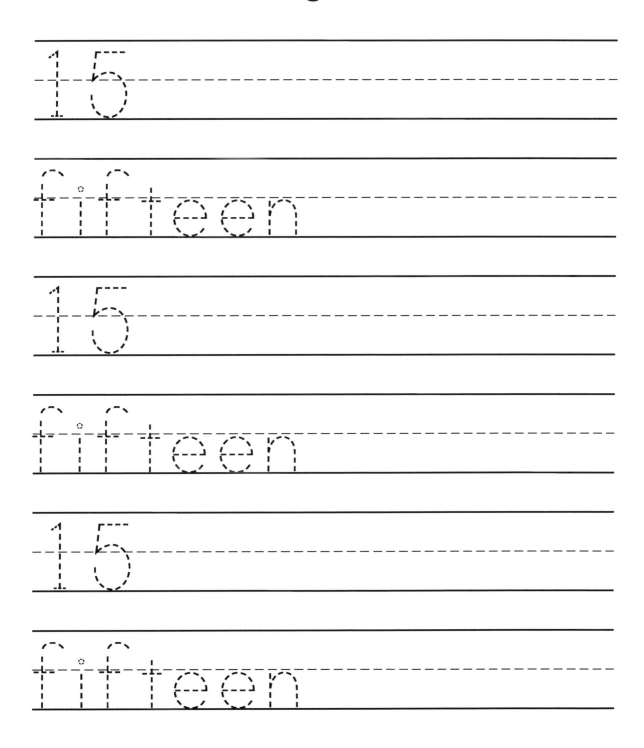

Trace the number 16.

16 16 16 16

sixteen sixteen

16 16 16 16

sixteen sixteen

16 16 16 16

sixteen sixteen

Trace the number 16.

16 16 16 16

sixteen sixteen

16 16 16 16

sixteen sixteen

16 16 16 16

sixteen sixteen

Practice writing the number 16.

16

sixteen

16

sixteen

16

sixteen

Practice writing the number 16.

16

sixteen

16

sixteen

16

sixteen

Trace the number 17.

17 17 17 17

seventeen

17 17 17 17

seventeen

17 17 17 17

seventeen

Trace the number 17.

17 17 17 17

seventeen

17 17 17 17

seventeen

17 17 17 17

seventeen

Practice writing the number 17.

17

seventeen

17

seventeen

17

seventeen

Practice writing the number 17.

17

seventeen

17

seventeen

17

seventeen

Trace the number 18.

18 18 18 18

eighteen eighteen

18 18 18 18

eighteen eighteen

18 18 18 18

eighteen eighteen

Trace the number 18.

18 18 18 18

eighteen eighteen

18 18 18 18

eighteen eighteen

18 18 18 18

eighteen eighteen

Practice writing the number 18.

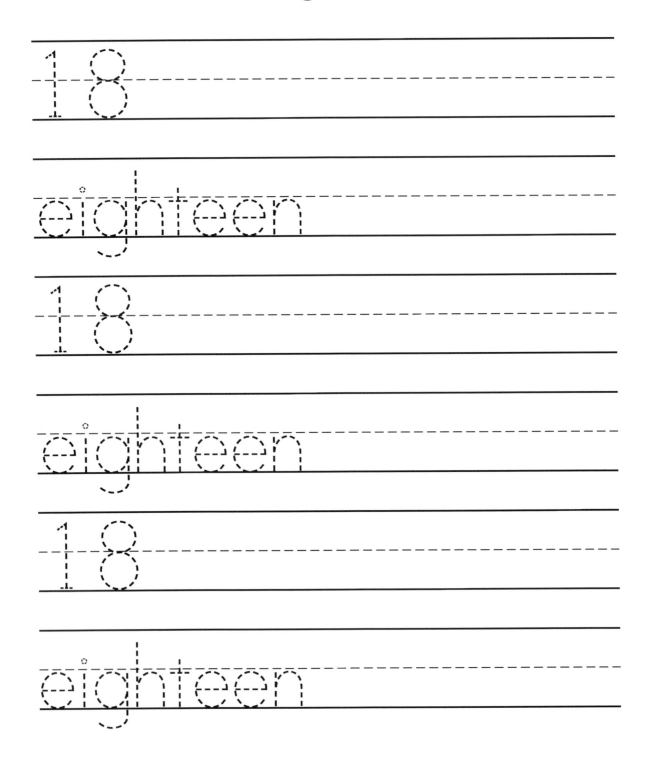

Practice writing the number 18.

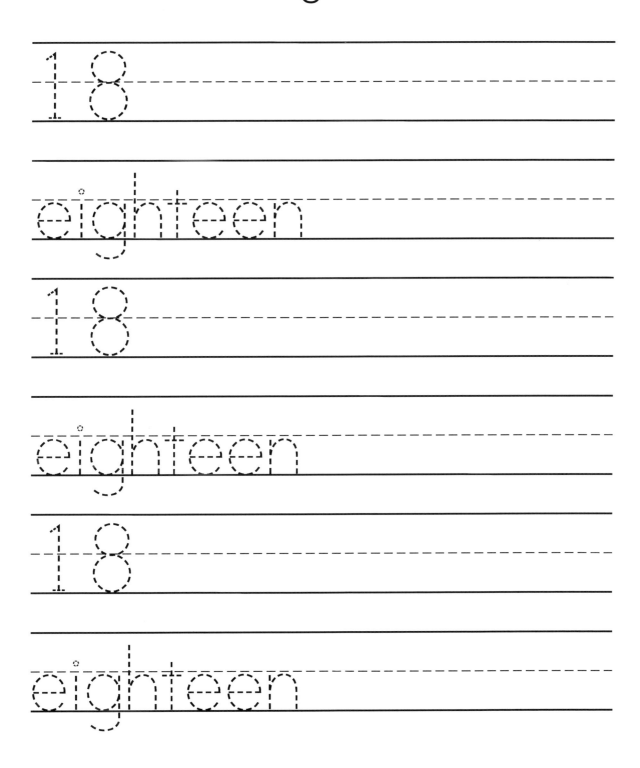

Trace the number 19.

19 19 19 19

nineteen nineteen

19 19 19 19

nineteen nineteen

19 19 19 19

nineteen nineteen

Trace the number 19.

19 19 19 19

nineteen nineteen

19 19 19 19

nineteen nineteen

19 19 19 19

nineteen nineteen

Practice writing the number 19.

19

nineteen

19

nineteen

19

nineteen

Practice writing the number 19.

19

nineteen

19

nineteen

19

nineteen

Trace the number 20.

20 20 20 20 20

twenty twenty

20 20 20 20 20

twenty twenty

20 20 20 20 20

twenty twenty

Trace the number 20.

20 20 20 20

twenty twenty

20 20 20 20

twenty twenty

20 20 20 20

twenty twenty

Practice writing the number 20.

20

twenty

20

twenty

20

twenty

Practice writing the number 20.

20

twenty

20

twenty

20

twenty

Printed in Great Britain
by Amazon